# Food for Festivals

## by Anne Witherington

### Co[ntents]

Chr[...] 2

Div[...] 4

Id-u[...] 6

Hin[...] 8

Pes[...] 10

Tha[...] 12

Sun[...] 14

Glo[...] 15

Ind[...] 16

Falkirk Council

LONGMAN

# Christmas

Christmas is the time when Christians celebrate Jesus's birthday. Many people have turkey to eat at Christmas. They have Christmas pudding and brandy butter or cream.

Christmas pudding

Mince pies

Ham

Vegetables

Turkey

Some people have Christmas dinner at a hotel or a restaurant. ➡

THE MANOR HOTEL
**CHRISTMAS DAY**
LUNCH FOR FAMILIES
◆
2 5 DECEMBER
◆

*Melon with blackcurrant sauce*
*Clear beef soup*
◆
*Traditionally stuffed roast turkey with braised chestnuts*
*Cranberry sauce*
*Roast potatoes*
*Brussels sprouts*
*Glazed carrots*
◆
*Vegetable and hazelnut crumble*
◆
*Christmas plum pudding, brandy butter, mince pies*
◆
*Yule log*
◆
*Coffee and mints*

**In the past people did not eat turkey at Christmas. They had boar's head, a peacock or maybe a swan.**

**They used to put trinkets or coins in plum puddings and mince pies for good luck. Plum puddings were made with dried fruit and nuts and cooked in a cloth.**

3

# Divali

Divali is a happy festival celebrated by Hindus and Sikhs. Lots of special food is eaten at Divali parties. The food has to be blessed before it is eaten.

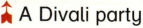 A Divali party

**Barfi – a fudge made from milk, sugar and nuts**

**Goojra – pasties filled with nuts and fruit**

**Puris – small puffed pancakes**

**Aloo bondas – spiced potato balls**

There are lots of lovely sweet dishes at Divali parties. These are made from flour, rice, sugar and many different sorts of nuts. There are wonderful savoury foods as well, like samosas, bhajis and tasty rice.

# Id-ul-Fitr

Many Muslims fast for
a month each year.
They do not eat or drink during the day.

Id-ul-Fitr is a
Muslim festival
to celebrate
the end of
the fast.

◄◄ Children have
new clothes
and presents for
Id-ul-Fitr.

The first food people eat at an Id party is a sweet pudding called sevian.

The women often make lots of special rice dishes and cook curry, kebabs, vegetables and puris.

Puris          Samosas          Sevian

Barfi          Soi Pita          Kebabs

Some of the food is the same as Divali food.

# Hina Matsuri:
# The Dolls' Festival

Japanese girls invite their friends to a party for the dolls' festival. The party guests eat hishimochi. These are rice cakes cut into diamond shapes.

This festival celebrates growing up and being healthy.

Special dolls are arranged on shelves.

⬆ Special food is put on the table for the party.

Sometimes Japanese girls in Britain have a Hina Matsuri party. A special cake is decorated with paper dolls and fruit.

The guests might have sushi to eat. In Britain sushi is usually made from rice, chicken or egg and red ginger, which is rolled up in seaweed and then dipped in a special sauce. In Japan raw fish is often used in sushi.

9

# Pesach: The Festival of Passover

Jewish people have a special meal for Pesach called the seder. They eat food which reminds them of a special time in their history.

Everyone drinks some wine or grape juice, eats **matzah** and tastes the food on the seder plate.

◄ Jews all over the world celebrate the Passover.

Everything on the **seder table** has a special meaning.

**The foods have many different flavours, some are bitter and some are sweet.**

burnt egg

roasted bone

bitter herbs

haroset

salt water

parsley

These are the foods on the seder plate.

# Thanksgiving

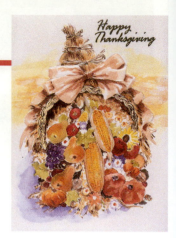

People in America have
a party for Thanksgiving.
They eat turkey and
**pumpkin** pie.

Thanksgiving is a thank-you for
a good harvest.

Sweet potatoes

Turkey and cranberry sauce

Corn muffins

Pumpkin pie

The first people to celebrate this festival were the settlers who went to America from Europe. They shared a big feast with the North American Indians. They ate venison, turkey, wild plums, nuts, berries and corn bread.

# Summary Chart of Festivals

| Festival | Who celebrates | Traditional food eaten |
|---|---|---|
| **Christmas** | Christians | Turkey, vegetables, Christmas pudding |
| **Divali** | Hindus, Sikhs | Samosas, bhajis, sweet dishes |
| **Id-ul-Fitr** | Muslims | Rice dishes, curry, kebabs, puris |
| **Hina Matsuri** | Japanese | Hishimochi (rice cakes) |
| **Pesach** | Jews | Matzah |
| **Thanksgiving** | North Americans | Turkey, sweet potatoes, pumpkin pie |

# Glossary of Words Used in This Book

**bhajis** *(page 5)*
A food made with batter and vegetables, shaped like a ball.

**curry** *(page 7)*
A sauce made with hot-tasting spices.

**haroset** *(page 11)*
A mixture of chopped nuts, grated apple, wine and cinnamon.

**kebabs** *(page 7)*
Meat and vegetables cooked on a stick.

**matzah** *(page 10)*
A special bread eaten at Pesach. It is baked without raising agent, so the bread stays flat like a cracker.

**pumpkin** *(page 12)*
A large round fruit. It is orange and is used in pies.

**samosas** *(page 5)*
Meat or vegetables covered with pastry.

**seder table** *(page 11)*
A table that has been set in a special way for the Pesach meal.

**soi pita** *(page 7)*
Pastry shapes made with rice flour, salt and water. They are then steam-cooked and eaten with curry or fried with onion.

**trinkets** *(page 3)*
Small objects.

**venison** *(page 13)*
The meat from a deer.

# Index

aloo bondas  5

barfi  5, 7

cake  9
chicken  9
Christians  2–3, 14
Christmas  2–3, 14
curry  7, 14

fruit  3, 5, 9

goojra  5

Hindu  4, 14

Id-ul-Fitr  6–7, 14

kebabs  7, 14

matzah  10, 14
Muslims  6, 14

Passover  10–11
Pesach  10–11, 14
pumpkin pie  12, 13, 14
puris  5, 7, 14

nuts  3, 5, 13

rice  5, 7, 8, 9, 14

samosas  5, 7, 14
seder  10, 11
sevian  7
Sikhs  4, 14
soi pita  7
sushi  9

Thanksgiving  12–13, 14
turkey  2, 3, 12, 13, 14

vegetables  2, 7, 14